Vesey Surname

Ireland: 1600s to 1900s

From Ireland Church Records of Baptism, Marriage and Death

Comprised of Roman Catholic and Church of Ireland Records

From Counties Carlow, Cork, Kerry and Dublin City

Compiled by **Donovan Hurst**

April 9, 2013

ISBN: 1939958164
ISBN-13: 978-1-939958-16-7

Dedication

This work is dedicated to all of those that came before us and shaped our lives to make us the people that we are today.

Table of Contents

Introduction

This is a compilation of individuals who have the surname of Vesey that lived in the country of Ireland from the 1600s to the 1900s. I have placed each entry into one of four categories: Families, Individual Births/Baptisms, Individual Burials, and Individual Marriages. If a marriage entry primarily concerns an Individual Vesey whom is female, then I have placed that entry under the category of Individual Marriages. If a marriage entry primarily concerns an Individual Vesey whom is male, then I have placed that entry under the category of Families. Images of many of these listings are available at http://churchrecords.irishgenealogy.ie/churchrecords/.

To help guide the reader of this work, the format of this book is as follows:

- Main Family Entry (Husband and Wife) (Father and Mother)

  - Child of Main Family Entry, including Spouse(s) when available

    - Grandchild of Main Family Entry, including Spouse(s) when available

      - Great-Grandchild of Main Family Entry, including Spouse(s) when available

(Bolded Text) following any entry includes any additional information such as Residence(s), Occupation(s), Signature(s), etc. when available.

Hurst

Some of the fonts used in this work symbolizes Celtic writing. The traditional letters, numbers, and punctuation marks and their Celtic counterparts are as follows:

Traditional Letters (Uppercase & Lowercase)

A a B b C c D d E f G g H h I i J j K k L l M m N n O o P p Q q R r S s T t U u V v W w X x Y y Z z

Celtic Letters (Uppercase & Lowercase)

A a B b C c D ð E e F f G g H h I i J j K k L l M m

N n O o P p Q q R r S s T t U u V v W w X x Y y Z z

Traditional Numbers

1 2 3 4 5 6 7 8 9 10

Celtic Numbers

1 2 3 4 5 6 7 8 9 10

Traditional Punctuation

. , : ' " & - ( )

Celtic Punctuation

. , : ' " & - ( )

Vesey Surname Ireland: 1600s to 1900s

Parish Churches

Carlow (Church of Ireland)

Dunleckney Parish.

Cork & Ross

(Roman Catholic or RC)

Cork -South Parish and Courcy's Country or Ballinspittal Parish.

Dublin (Church of Ireland)

Lucan Park Parish, Rotunda Chapel Parish, St. Anne Parish, St. Bride Parish, St. George Parish, St. James Parish, St. Luke Parish, St. Mark Parish, St. Mary Parish, St. Michan Parish, St. Nicholas Without Parish, St. Paul Parish, St. Peter Parish, St. Stephen Parish, and St. Thomas Parish.

Dublin (Roman Catholic or RC)

Rathfarnham Parish, SS. Michael & John Parish, St. Agatha Parish, St. Andrew Parish, St. Catherine Parish, St. James Parish, St. Mary, Haddington Road Parish, St. Mary, Pro Cathedral Parish, St. Michan Parish, and St. Nicholas Parish.

Kerry (Roman Catholic or RC)

Annascaul Parish.

Families

- Agmundishan Vesey & Jane Vesey

  o George Vesey – bapt. 26 Apr 1719 (Baptism, St. Paul Parish)

- Edward Vesey & Frances Vesey

  o Jane Vesey – bapt. 9 Oct 1742 (Baptism, St. Mary Parish)

- George Vesey & Catherine Vesey

  o James Vesey – bapt. 21 Oct 1781 (Baptism, St. Luke Parish)

George Vesey (father):

Residence - Crooked Staff - October 21, 1781

Occupation - Weaver - October 21, 1781

Hurst

- George Vesey & Unknown

  - Thomas Agmon Vesey & Frances Blakeney – 19 Sep 1865 (Marriage, **St. Stephen Parish**)

Signatures:

Signatures (Marriages):

Thomas Agmon Vesey (son):

  Residence - Lawrence Town, Ballinastoe - September 19, 1865

  Occupation - M. B. - September 19, 1865

Frances Blakeney, daughter of John Blakeney (daughter-in-law):

  Residence - 42 Pembroke Road - September 19, 1865

  Occupation - M. B. - September 19, 1865

2

Vesey Surname Ireland: 1600s to 1900s

John Blakeney (father):

   Occupation - Solicitor

George Vesey (father):

   Occupation - Clerk in Holy Orders

Wedding Witnesses:

Robert Stephens & Dodwell J. G. Browne

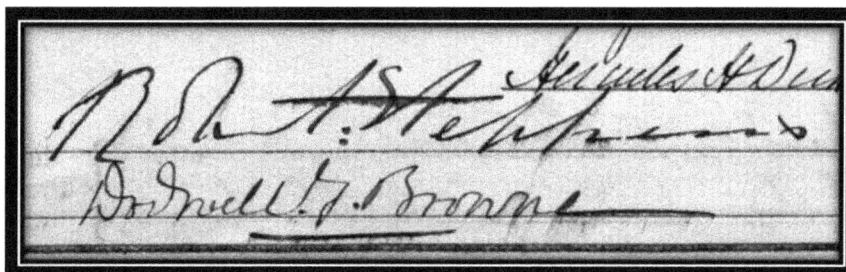

Signatures:

- Gulielmo Vesey & Catherine Unknown

    o Richard Vesey – bapt. 1755 (Baptism, **St. Andrew Parish** (RC))

- Hamilton Vesey & Jane Roche

    o John Vesey – bapt. 12 Sep 1841 (Baptism, **St. James Parish** (RC))

- James Vesey & Alice Styles – 14 Sep 1839 (Marriage, **St. James Parish** (RC))

    o James Vesey – bapt. 18 Mar 1841 (Baptism, **St. James Parish** (RC))

Wedding Witnesses:

Andrew Cullen & Anne Kennedy

- James Vesey & Anne Unknown

    o Mary Anne Vesey – bapt. 1836 (Baptism, **St. Andrew Parish** (RC))

Hurst

- James Vesey & Catherine Lynch

  o Esther Vesey – bapt. 29 Mar 1790 (Baptism, **St. Catherine Parish (RC)**)

- James Vesey & Elizabeth Dolstram – 28 Sep 1736 (Marriage, **St. Mark Parish**)

  o Mary Vesey – bapt. 6 Jul 1737 (Baptism, **St. Mark Parish**)

  o Fairbanks Vesey – bapt. 11 Sep 1739 (Baptism, **St. Mark Parish**)

  o William Vesey – bapt. 5 Jul 1742 (Baptism, **St. Mark Parish**)

  o Christian Vesey (Daughter) – bapt. 29 Jul 1745 (Baptism, **St. Mark Parish**)

  o Richard Raphson Vesey – bapt. 26 Jan 1747 (Baptism, **St. Mark Parish**)

James Vesey (father):

Residence - White's Quay - July 6, 1737

July 5, 1742

July 29, 1745

January 26, 1747

George's Quay - September 11, 1739

- James Vesey & Frances Vesey

  o Elizabeth Vesey – b. 12 Apr 1866, bapt. 15 Apr 1866 (Baptism, **St. Mary Parish**)

James Vesey (father):

Residence - 10 Marlboro Street - April 15, 1866

Occupation - Book Binder - April 15, 1866

Vesey Surname Ireland: 1600s to 1900s

- John Vesey & Catherine Murphy
  - John Vesey – b. 4 May 1858, bapt. 5 May 1858 (Baptism, **St. Mary, Pro Cathedral Parish (RC)**)

John Vesey (father):

Residence - 8 Britain Court - May 5, 1858

- John Vesey & Catherine Unknown
  - John Vesey & Sarah Smyth – 4 Jan 1880 (Marriage, **St. Mary, Haddington Road Parish (RC)**)
    - John Vesey – b. 14 Mar 1880, bapt. 22 Mar 1880 (Baptism, **St. Mary, Haddington Road Parish (RC)**)

John Vesey (son):

Residence - 22 Irishtown Road - January 4, 1880

March 22, 1880

Sarah Smyth, daughter of John Smyth & Elizabeth Unknown (daughter-in-law):

Residence - 3 Thomas Street, Ring's End - January 4, 1880

Wedding Witnesses:

Gulielmo Cox & Mary Locke

- John Vesey & Cecelia Walsh
  - Anne Vesey – bapt. 18 Feb 1806 (Baptism, **Cork - South Parish (RC)**)

Hurst

- John Vesey & Elizabeth Lynch – 9 Dec 1746 (Marriage, **St. Mary Parish**)

John Vesey (husband):

    Residence - Guam - December 9, 1746

    Occupation - Reverend - December 9, 1746

- John Vesey & Frances Unknown
  - Thomas Vesey – bapt. 20 Sep 1803 (Baptism, **St. Peter Parish**)

John Vesey (father):

    Residence - Merrion Square - September 20, 1803

- John Vesey & Marcia Unknown
  - Elizabeth Vesey – bapt. 1845 (Baptism, **St. Andrew Parish (RC)**)
- John Vesey & Mary Short
  - Mary Anne Vesey – b. 20 May 1882, bapt. 22 May 1882 (Baptism, **St. Michan Parish (RC)**)
  - Ellen Vesey – b. 4 Aug 1885, bapt. 7 Aug 1885 (Baptism, **St. Mary, Pro Cathedral Parish (RC)**)
  - Catherine Vesey – b. 12 Jul 1887, bapt. 18 Jul 1887 (Baptism, **St. Mary, Pro Cathedral Parish (RC)**)
  - Thomas Vesey – b. 18 Aug 1889, bapt. 26 Aug 1889 (Baptism, **St. Mary, Pro Cathedral Parish (RC)**)
  - William Vesey – b. 16 Nov 1891, bapt. 18 Nov 1891 (Baptism, **St. Mary, Pro Cathedral Parish (RC)**)
  - James Joseph Vesey – b. 21 Aug 1895, bapt. 23 Aug 1895 (Baptism, **St. Mary, Pro Cathedral Parish (RC)**)

Vesey Surname Ireland: 1600s to 1900s

- Margaret Vesey – b. 15 Sep 1897, bapt. 20 Sep 1897 (Baptism, **St. Mary, Pro Cathedral Parish (RC)**)

- Anne Vesey – b. 9 Aug 1899, bapt. 11 Aug 1899 (Baptism, **St. Mary, Pro Cathedral Parish (RC)**)

John Vesey (father):

Residence - 5 Dispensary Lane - May 22, 1882

3 Moore Cottages - August 7, 1885

2 Kelly's Row - July 18, 1887

24 Kelly's Row - August 26, 1889

November 18, 1891

9 Kelly's Row - August 23, 1895

September 20, 1897

August 11, 1899

- John Vesey & Mary Unknown
  - Joan Vesey – bapt. 1831 (Baptism, **St. Andrew Parish** (RC))
  - Bridget Vesey – bapt. 1833 (Baptism, **St. Andrew Parish** (RC))
  - William Vesey – bapt. 1837 (Baptism, **St. Andrew Parish** (RC))
  - Joseph Vesey – bapt. 1839 (Baptism, **St. Andrew Parish** (RC))

Hurst

- John Stuart Vesey & Unknown

  o Elizabeth Mary Vesey (1st Marriage) & Unknown Armstrong (A r m s t r o n g)

  o Elizabeth Mary Vesey Armstrong (A r m s t r o n g) (2nd Marriage) & William Dowman – 18 Aug 1888 (Marriage, St. Stephen Parish)

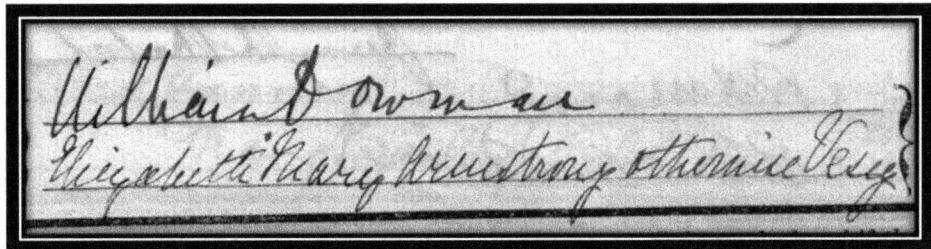

Signatures:

Elizabeth Mary Vesey Armstrong (daughter):

   Residence - Ballymena, Co. Antrim - August 18, 1888

   Relationship Status at 2nd Marriage - widow

William Dowman, son of Jonathan Darby Dowman (son-in-law)

   Residence - 89 Lower Mount Street - August 18, 1888

   Occupation - Late Captain, 40th Regiment - August 18, 1888

   Relationship Status at Marriage - widow

Jonathan Darby Dowman (father):

   Occupation - Retired Officer, H. M. S.

John Stuart Vesey (father):

   Occupation - Esquire, Medical Doctor

Vesey Surname Ireland: 1600s to 1900s

Wedding Witnesses:

Lucy Elizabeth Vesey & John Rubina Gaussen

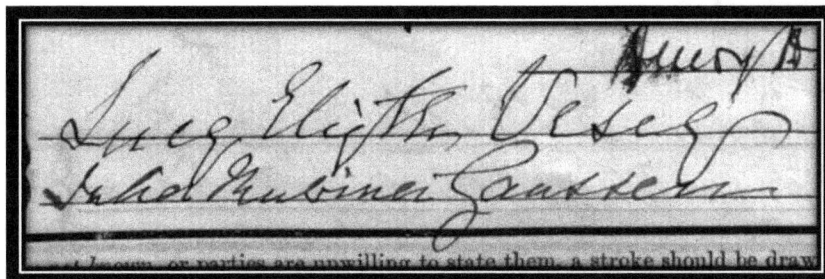

Signatures:

- Julian Vesey & Catherine Unknown

    o Lewis Vesey – b. 1749, bapt. 1749 (Baptism, **St. Andrew Parish (RC)**)

    o John Vesey – bapt. 1758 (Baptism, **St. Andrew Parish (RC)**)

    o Peter Vesey – bapt. 1760 (Baptism, **St. Andrew Parish (RC)**)

    o Lewis Vesey – bapt. 1762 (Baptism, **St. Andrew Parish (RC)**)

    o Frances or Francis – bapt. 1763 (Baptism, **St. Andrew Parish (RC)**)

    o Joseph Vesey – bapt. 1765 (Baptism, **St. Andrew Parish (RC)**)

    o Simon Vesey – bapt. 1766 (Baptism, **St. Andrew Parish (RC)**)

- Luke Vesey & Elizabeth Unknown

    o Luke Vesey – bapt. 3 Mar 1825 (Baptism, **St. Mary, Pro Cathedral Parish (RC)**)

Luke Vesey (father):

Residence - Moor Street - March 3, 1825

Hurst

- McMilton Vesey & Jane Unknown

  - William Vesey – b. 14 May 1839, bapt. 26 May 1839 (Baptism, **St. James Parish**)

McMilton Vesey (father):

Residence - Echlin Street - May 26, 1839

Occupation - Smith - May 26, 1839

- Patrick Vesey & Anne Daly

  - Mary Teresa Vesey – b. 1876, bapt. 1876 (Baptism, **St. Andrew Parish (RC)**)

Patrick Vesey (father):

Residence - 188 Townsend Street - 1876

- Patrick Vesey & Honor Dunn

  - Patrick Vesey – bapt. 15 Jun 1800 (Baptism, **St. Catherine Parish (RC)**)

- Patrick Vesey & Margaret Brewton

  - Mary Vesey – bapt. 23 Jun 1847 (Baptism, **St. Nicholas Parish (RC)**)

- Patrick Vesey & Margaret Brienton – 10 Jan 1830 (Marriage, **St. Andrew Parish (RC)**)

  - Michael Vesey – bapt. 9 Jan 1835 (Baptism, **SS. Michael & John Parish (RC)**)

  - Margaret Vesey – bapt. 18 Mar 1838 (Baptism, **SS. Michael & John Parish (RC)**)

  - Patrick Vesey – bapt. 20 Oct 1839 (Baptism, **SS. Michael & John Parish (RC)**)

  - Joseph Vesey – bapt. 28 Nov 1844 (Baptism, **SS. Michael & John Parish (RC)**)

Wedding Witnesses:

Michael Vesey & Anne Vesey

Vesey Surname Ireland: 1600s to 1900s

- Patrick Vesey & Margaret Farrell

  o James Vesey – bapt. 15 Jan 1769 (Baptism, **St. Catherine Parish** (RC))

  o Mary Vesey – bapt. 5 Jan 1774 (Baptism, **St. Catherine Parish** (RC))

  o Francis Vesey – bapt. 14 Jan 1776 (Baptism, **St. Catherine Parish** (RC))

  o John Vesey – bapt. 7 Jul 1782 (Baptism, **St. Catherine Parish** (RC))

- Patrick Vesey & Margaret Unknown

  o Mary Vesey & Christopher Casey – 23 Feb 1868 (Marriage, **St. Andrew Parish** (RC))

    ▪ Elizabeth Casey – b. 1868, bapt. 1868 (Baptism, **St. Andrew Parish** (RC))

    ▪ Mary Casey – b. 23 Oct 1873, bapt. 27 Oct 1873 (Baptism, **St. Nicholas Parish** (RC))

    ▪ Matilda Casey – b. 1877, bapt. 1877 (Baptism, **St. Andrew Parish** (RC))

    ▪ Christine Casey – b. 1878, bapt. 1879 (Baptism, **St. Andrew Parish** (RC))

Mary Vesey (daughter):

Residence - 27 Essex Street - February 23, 1868

Christopher Casey, son of Patrick Casey & Elizabeth Unknown (son-in-law):

Residence - 25 Essex Street - February 23, 1868

51 Clarendon Street - 1868

7 Peter's Row - October 27, 1873

8 Stephen's Place - 1877

1879

Wedding Witnesses:

Christopher Kelly & Margaret Wilson

Hurst

- Patrick Vesey & Sarah White

  - Sarah Vesey – b. 1790, bapt. 1790 (Baptism, **SS. Michael & John Parish (RC)**)

- Patrick Vesey & Susan Hart – 19 Nov 1838 (Marriage, **St. Nicholas Parish (RC)**)

  - Margaret Vesey & Patrick O'Connor – 7 Sep 1885 (Marriage, **St. Mary, Pro Cathedral Parish (RC)**)

    - Mary Anne O'Connor – b. 19 Mar 1886, bapt. 24 May 1886 (Baptism, **St. Mary, Pro Cathedral Parish (RC)**)

    - Margaret O'Connor – b. 17 Mar 1887, bapt. 21 Mar 1887 (Baptism, **St. Mary, Pro Cathedral Parish (RC)**)

    - Esther O'Connor – b. 28 Mar 1888, bapt. 4 Apr 1888 (Baptism, **St. Mary, Pro Cathedral Parish (RC)**)

    - Patrick O'Connor – b. 26 Nov 1889, bapt. 6 Dec 1889 (Baptism, **St. Agatha Parish (RC)**)

    - Christopher O'Connor – b. 23 Dec 1891, bapt. 29 Dec 1891 (Baptism, **St. Agatha Parish (RC)**)

Margaret Vesey (daughter):

Residence - 5 Langrish Place - September 7, 1885

Patrick O'Connor, son of Patrick O'Connor & Anne Troy (son-in-law):

Residence - 5 Langrish Place - September 7, 1885

May 24, 1886

March 21, 1887

9 North Gloster Place - April 4, 1888

21 Summer Hill Street - December 6, 1889

21 Summer Hill Parade - December 29, 1891

Vesey Surname Ireland: 1600s to 1900s

Wedding Witnesses to marriage between Margaret Vesey & Patrick O'Connor:

Thomas Brogan & Elizabeth Doyle

Wedding Witnesses to marriage between Patrick Vesey & Susan Hart:

Michael Worth & Margaret Vesey

- Thomas Vesey & Jane Vesey

    o Elizabeth Vesey – bapt. 18 Apr 1765 (Baptism, St. Mary Parish)

    o John Vesey – bapt. 18 Mar 1768 (Baptism, St. Mark Parish)

Thomas Vesey (father):

   Residence - York Street - March 18, 1768

- Thomas Vesey & Margaret Burn (B u r n) – 24 Jul 1676 (Marriage, St. Bride Parish)
- Thomas Vesey & Unknown

    o Thomas Vesey & Ellen Marsden – 7 Nov 1859 (Marriage, St. Peter Parish)

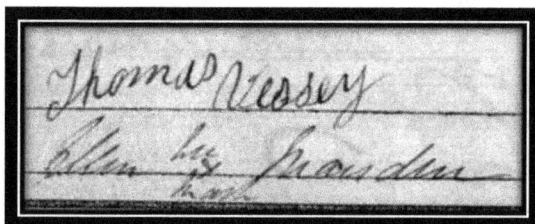

Signatures:

     ▪ Ellen Anne Vesey – b. 20 Sep 1858, bapt. 20 Sep 1858 (Baptism, St. Peter Parish)

Thomas Vesey (son):

   Residence - Newbridge - September 20, 1858

   Portobello Barracks - November 7, 1859

Hurst

Occupation - Private, Royal Horse Artillery - September 20, 1858

Gunner, Royal Artillery - November 7, 1859

Ellen Marsden, daughter of James Marsden (daughter-in-law):

Residence - Portobello Barracks - November 7, 1859

James Marsden (father):

Occupation - Stone Mason

Thomas Vesey (father):

Occupation - Sailor

Wedding Witnesses:

Sarah Jane Daveys & Arthur Curran

Signatures:

- Unknown Vesey & Mary Unknown
  - Richard Vesey – b. 16 Apr 1876, bapt. 5 May 1876 (Baptism, **St. Mary, Pro Cathedral Parish (RC)**)

- Unknown Vesey & Unknown

  o Almon B. Vesey

Signature:

- Unknown Vesey & Unknown

  o George Vesey

Signature:

- Unknown Vesey & Unknown

  o Richard Murray Vesey

Signature:

Hurst

- Unknown Vesey & Unknown
  - William M. Vesey

Signature:

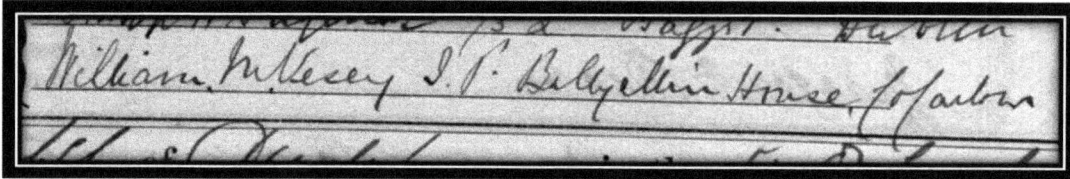

- William Vesey & Unknown Authom – 29 Dec 1720 (Marriage, **St. Peter Parish**)

William Vesey (husband):

Occupation - Esquire - December 29, 1720

Unknown Authom (wife):

Occupation - Lady - December 29, 1720

- William John Vesey & Isabella Elizabeth Brownlow – 27 Jul 1837 (Marriage, **St. Peter Parish**)

William John Vesey (husband):

Residence - Abbeyliex - July 27, 1837

Isabella Elizabeth Brownlow (wife):

Residence - 29 Merrion Square - July 27, 1837

Wedding Witnesses:

Unknown McFrouder & Albert Nugent

Individual Baptisms/Births

- Elizabeth Vesey – b. 12 Apr 1866, bapt. 15 Apr 1866 (Baptism, **Rotunda Chapel Parish**)

Elizabeth Vesey (child):

> **Residence - Ward 4 - April 15, 1866**

- Esther Vesey – bapt. 16 Apr 1732 (Baptism, **St. Paul Parish**), bur. 2 May 1732 (Burial, **St. Paul Parish**)

Easter Vesey (child):

> **Age at Baptism - child**

> **Age at Death - child**

- Henry Vesey – bapt. 27 Apr 1732 (Baptism, **St. Paul Parish**)

Henry Vesey (child):

> **Age at Baptism - child**

Individual Burials

- Catherine Vesey – bur. 9 Oct 1729 (Burial, **St. Paul Parish**)

Catherine Vesey (deceased):

    Age at Death - child

- Catherine Vesey – bur. 20 Jan 1808 (Burial, **St. Peter Parish**)

Catherine Vesey (deceased):

    Residence - Aungier Street - before January 20, 1808

- Charles Coldurst Vesey – b. 1826, d. 15 May 1885, bur. 1885 (Burial, **Lucan Parish**)

Charles Coldurst Vesey (deceased):

    Residence - Lucan House - May 15, 1885

    Age at Death - 59 years

- Charlotte Vesey – b. 20 Dec 1874, bur. 21 Dec 1874 (Burial, **Dunleckney Parish**)

Charlotte Vesey (deceased):

    Residence - Ballyellan House - before December 21, 1874

    Age at Death - 1 day

Vesey Surname Ireland: 1600s to 1900s

- Denny Vesey – bur. 22 Apr 1700 (Burial, **St. Michan Parish**)

Denny Vesey (deceased):

    Relationship Status at Death - bachelor

- Elizabeth Vesey – b. 1806, bur. 26 Jun 1832 (Burial, **St. Mark Parish**)

Elizabeth Vesey (deceased):

    Residence - Ring's End - before June 26, 1832

    Age at Death - 26 years

- Elizabeth Vesey – b. 1775, bur. 1 Oct 1820 (Burial, **St. Peter Parish**)

Elizabeth Vesey (deceased):

    Residence - Cuffe Street - before October 1, 1820

    Age at Death - 45 years

    Place of Burial - St. Kevin's Church Yard

- Frances Vesey – bur. 20 Feb 1743 (Burial, **St. Mary Parish**)

Frances Vesey (deceased):

    Age at Death - child

- George Vesey – bur. 12 Aug 1816 (Burial, **St. Mary Parish**)

George Vesey (deceased):

    Residence - Phibsborough - before August 12, 1816

Hurst

- Grace Vesey – bur. 29 Sep 1819 (Burial, **St. Mary Parish**)

Grace Vesey (deceased):

    Residence - Phibsborough - before September 29, 1819

    Relationship Status at Death - Mrs.

- Joseph Vesey – bur. 22 Nov 1798 (Burial, **St. James Parish**)

Joseph Vesey (deceased):

    Residence - Custom House - before November 22, 1798

- Mary Vesey – bur. 8 Jun 1712 (Burial, **St. Nicholas Without Parish**)

Mary Vesey (deceased):

    Residence - Patrick Street - before June 8, 1712

- Mary Vesey – bur. 5 May 1731 (Burial, **St. Paul Parish**)

Mary Vesey (deceased):

    Age at Death - child

- Mary Vesey – bur. 24 May 1743 (Burial, **St. Mark Parish**)
- Mary Vesey – d. 11 Oct 1835, bur. 1835 (Burial, **St. James Parish**)

Mary Vesey (deceased):

    Residence - Echlin Street - October 11, 1835

Vesey Surname Ireland: 1600s to 1900s

- Mary Vesey – b. 1831, d. 25 Feb 1855, bur. 1855 (Burial, **St. James Parish**)

Mary Vesey (deceased):

Residence - North Brunswick Street - February 25, 1855

Age at Death - 24 years

- Mary Jane Vesey – b. 1842, d. 2 Jan 1851, bur. 1851 (Burial, **St. James Parish**)

Mary Jane Vesey (deceased):

Residence - Echlin Street - January 2, 1851

Age at Death - 9 years

- Patrick Vesey – bur. 1 May 1812 (Burial, **St. James Parish**)

Patrick Vesey (deceased):

Residence - Tighe Street - before May 1, 1812

- Robert Vesey – bur. 28 Jan 1714 (Burial, **St. Paul Parish**)
- Susanna Vesey – b. 1800, bur. 22 May 1831 (Burial, **St. Mark Parish**)

Susanna Vesey (deceased):

Residence - Ring's End - before May 22, 1831

Age at Death - 31 years

- Thomas Vesey – bur. 29 Feb 1812 (Burial, **St. James Parish**)

Thomas Vesey (deceased):

Residence - Tighe Street - before February 29, 1812

Hurst

- Unknown Vesey – b. 1757, bur. 8 Mar 1817 (Burial, **St. Peter Parish**)

Unknown Vesey (deceased):

    Age at Death - 60 years

- Unknown Vesey (Miss) – bur. 9 Feb 1744 (Burial, **St. Mary Parish**)

- Unknown Vesey (Mr.) – bur. 2 May 1743 (Burial, **St. Mary Parish**)

Unknown Vesey (Mr.) (deceased):

    Occupation - Lieutenant - before May 2, 1743

- Unknown Vesey (Mr.) – bur. 8 Apr 1750 (Burial, **St. Mary Parish**)

Unknown Vesey (Mr.) (deceased):

    Occupation - Doctor - before April 8, 1750

- Unknown Vesey (Mrs.) – bur. 29 May 1766

Unknown Vesey (Mrs.) (deceased):

    Residence - Henry Street - before May 29, 1766

Individual Marriages

- Anne Vesey & Edmond Weld – 25 Oct 1771 (Marriage, **St. Anne Parish**)

Edmond Weld (husband):

    Occupation - Esquire - October 25, 1771

- Anne Vesey & James Callaghan – 8 Jan 1745 (Marriage, **St. Catherine Parish (RC)**)

Wedding Witnesses:

Charles McCarty & Richard Giraghty

- Anne Vesey & Michael Magennis – 7 May 1844 (Marriage, **SS. Michael & John Parish (RC)**)

Wedding Witnesses:

Thomas Vesey & M. Combe

- Bridget Vesey & James O'Driscoll – 25 Apr 1911 (Marriage, **Annascaul Parish (RC)**)

James O'Driscoll, son of John O'Driscoll & Mary Bowler.

- Catherine Vesey & Michael Moylan
    - Mary Jane Moylan – b. 16 May 1875, bapt. 26 May 1875 (Baptism, **St. Mary, Pro Cathedral Parish (RC)**)

Michael Moylan (father):

Residence - 22 Lower Temple Street - May 26, 1875

Hurst

- Eleanor Vesey & Edward Tobin – 3 Dec 1813 (Marriage, **St. Catherine Parish** (RC))

  o Elizabeth Tobin – bapt. 6 Dec 1821 (Baptism, **St. Catherine Parish** (RC))

Wedding Witnesses:

Anthony Daly & Eleanor Dalton

- Eleanor Vesey & Samuel Heap – 16 Apr 1750 (Marriage, **St. Paul Parish**)

- Eleanor Vesey & Thomas Seary

  o Patrick Seary – b. 8 Jun 1873, bapt. 10 Jun 1873 (Baptism, **St. James Parish** (RC))

  o John Seary – b. 4 Aug 1875, bapt. 7 Aug 1875 (Baptism, **St. Catherine Parish** (RC))

  o Charles Joseph Seary – b. 11 Feb 1879, bapt. Feb 1879 (Baptism, **St. Catherine Parish** (RC))

Thomas Seary (father):

Residence - Basin Lane - June 10, 1873

127 Thomas Street - August 7, 1875

February 1879

- Elizabeth Vesey & Patrick Ewing – 1 Oct 1809 (Marriage, **St. Catherine Parish** (RC))

  o Emily Ewing – bapt. 17 Aug 1810 (Baptism, **St. James Parish** (RC))

  o George Ewing – bapt. 10 Aug 1812 (Baptism, **St. James Parish** (RC))

  o Patrick James Joseph Ewing – bapt. 5 Aug 1816 (Baptism, **St. James Parish** (RC))

Wedding Witnesses:

William Yore, John Brennan, & Jane Farrell

- Elizabeth Vesey & Richard Dawson – 25 Feb 1723 (Marriage, **St. Anne Parish**)

- Frances Vesey & Robert Marshall – 2 May 1788 (Marriage, **St. Anne Parish**)

Vesey Surname Ireland: 1600s to 1900s

- Jane Vesey & Henry Barry Knox – 30 Sep 1841 (Marriage, **St. George Parish**)

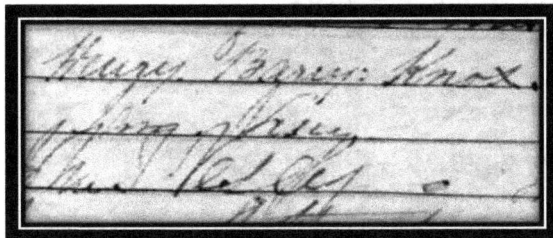

Signatures:

Jane Vesey (wife):

　　Residence - St. George Parish - September 30, 1841

Henry Barry Knox (husband):

　　Residence - Hadleigh Parish, Suffolk County, England - September 30, 1841

　　Occupation - Reverend - September 30, 1841

Wedding Witnesses:

John J. Vesey, John Tisdall, & Thomas Rothwell

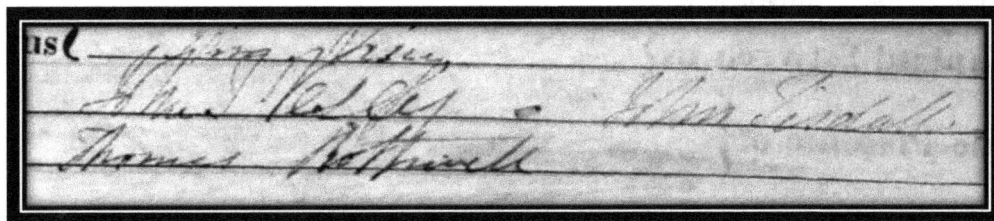

Signatures:

- Julia Vesey & William Barrett
  - William Patrick Barrett – b. 25 Aug 1861, bapt. 4 Sep 1861 (Baptism, **St. Nicholas Parish** (RC))
  - Unknown [Hard to Read] Barrett – b. 11 Sep 1864, bapt. 19 Sep 1864 (Baptism, **St. Nicholas Parish** (RC))
  - Margaret Barrett – b. 21 Dec 1866, bapt. 31 Dec 1866 (Baptism, **St. Nicholas Parish** (RC))

Hurst

William Barrett (father):

    Residence - **27 Bishop Street** - **September 4, 1861**

    7 [Hard to Read] - **September 19, 1864**

    38 White Street - **December 31, 1866**

- Margaret Vesey & Edward Donagh – 29 Nov 1838 (Marriage, **St. Nicholas Parish** (RC))

Wedding Witnesses:

Patrick Byrne & Sarah D'Arcy

- Margaret Vesey & Edward Donogh – 2 Jul 1843 (Marriage, **Rathfarnham Parish** (RC))

Wedding Witnesses:

Patrick Carroll & Anne Carroll

- Mary Vesey & Henry Ellis – 9 Dec 1758 (Marriage, **St. Anne Parish**)

Mary Vesey (wife):

    Relationship Status at Marriage - **Mrs.**

Henry Ellis (husband):

    Occupation - Esquire - **December 9, 1758**

- Mary Vesey & John Ladaveze – 26 Jan 1788 (Marriage, **St. Anne Parish**)

John Ladaveze (husband):

    Occupation - Esquire - **January 26, 1788**

Vesey Surname Ireland: 1600s to 1900s

- Mary Vesey & Michael Kilfoyle

  - Michael Kilfoyle – b. 12 Sep 1823, bapt. 15 Sep 1823 (Baptism, **St. Catherine Parish (RC)**)

- Mary Vesey & Timothy Carthy – 15 Feb 1836 (Marriage, **Courcy's Country or Ballinspittal Parish (RC)**)

- Mary Jane Vesey & Robert Ellwood – 31 Mar 1814 (Marriage, **St. James Parish**)

Robert Ellwood (husband):

Residence - Ballymore, Co. Roscommon - March 31, 1814

Occupation - Esquire - March 31, 1814

Name Variations

Includes Latin and Abbreviated forms of names found in the original documents.

Abigail = Abigale, Abigall

Anne = Ann, Anna, Annae

Bartholomew = Barth, Bartholmeus, Bartholomeo

Bridget = Birgis, Brigid, Brigida, Bridgit

Catherine = Catharine, Catharina, Catharinae, Catherina, Cath, Catha, Cathae, Cathe, Cathn, Kate

Charles = Carolus, Charls, Chas

Christopher = Christoph

Daniel = Danielem, Danielis

Edmund = Edmond

Edward = Ed, Edwd

Eleanor = Eleo, Eleonora, Elinor, Ellenor

Elizabeth = Betty, Elisa, Elisabeth, Eliz, Eliza, Elizab, Elizh, Elizth

Ellen = Elena, Ellena

Emily = Emilia

Esther = Essie, Ester

Francis = Fransicum

George = Geo, Georg, Georgius

Grace = Gratiae

Gulielmo = Guil, Guillelmi, Gulielmum, Guillelmus, Gulmi

Helen = Helena

Vesey Surname Ireland: 1600s to 1900s

Honor = Hanora, Honora

James = Jacobi, Jacobus, Jas

Jane = Joanna

Jeanne = Jeannae, Joannae

Joan = Johanna, Joney

John = Jno, Joannem, Joannes, Johannis

Joseph = Jos

Juliana = Julian

Leticia = Letitia, Lettice, Letticia

Lewis = Louis

Luke = Lucas

Margaret = Margarita, Margaritae, Margeret, Marget, Margt

Martha = Marthae

Mary = Maria, My

Mary Anne = Marianna, Marianne, Maryanne

Michael = Michaelis, Michl

Patrick = Pat, Patt, Patk, Patricii, Patricius

Peter = Petri

Richard = Ricardi, Ricardus, Rich, Richd

Robert = Roberti

Rose = Rosa, Rosae

Thomas = Thom, Thomae, Thoms, Thos, Ths

Timothy = Timotheus, Timy

William = Wil, Will, Willm, Wm

Notes

Notes

Notes

Notes

Notes

Notes

Index

36

Vesey Surname Ireland: 1600s to 1900s

O

R

S

T

Vesey Surname Ireland: 1600s to 1900s

About The Author

Donovan Hurst graduated from San Diego State University with a Bachelor of Arts in the major field of studies of History and a minor in the field of studies of Anthropology. He is a current member of The General Society of Mayflower Descendants and has been conducting genealogical research for over 10 years tracing back his ancestors to their ancestral homelands in Denmark, England, France, Germany, Ireland, Norway, and Scotland.

www.ingramcontent.com/pod-product-compliance
Lightning Source LLC
Chambersburg PA
CBHW080056280326
41934CB00014B/3336